BLOWING
ON YOGURT
AND OTHER EGYPTIAN
ARABIC EXPRESSIONS

T0034061

BLOWING
ON YOGURT
AND OTHER EGYPTIAN
ARABIC EXPRESSIONS
Illi in Fifty Idioms

Mona Hassan
Nagwa Kassabgy

Illustrated by Noha Elfarouk

The American University in Cairo Press
Cairo   New York

First published in 2024 by
The American University in Cairo Press
113 Sharia Kasr el Aini, Cairo, Egypt
420 Lexington Avenue, Suite 1644, New York, NY 10170
www.aucpress.com

Copyright © 2024 by Mona Hassan and Nagwa Kassabgy

All rights reserved. No part of this publication may be reproduced, stored in a retrieval system, or transmitted in any form or by any means, electronic, mechanical, photocopying, recording, or otherwise, without the prior written permission of the publisher.

ISBN 978 1 649 03346 8

Library of Congress Cataloging-in-Publication Data applied for.

Names: Hassan, Mona Kamel, author. | Kassabgy, Nagwa, author.
Title: Blowing on yogurt and other Egyptian Arabic expressions : illi
   in fifty idioms / Mona Hassan, Nagwa Kassabgy.
Identifiers: LCCN 2023035152 | ISBN 9781649033468 (hardback)
| ISBN
   9781649033475 (adobe pdf)
Subjects: LCSH: Arabic language--Egypt--Idioms. | Arabic
   language--Dialects--Egypt--Textbooks for foreign speakers--En-
glish. |
   Arabic language--Textbooks for foreign speakers--English.
Classification: LCC PJ6779 .H37 2024 | DDC 492.783421--dc23/
eng/20231206

1 2 3 4 5   28 27 26 25 24

Designed by David G. Hanna

Contents

Introduction

This book showcases and explains fifty frequently used Egyptian colloquial idiomatic expressions and proverbs that begin with the relative pronoun *2illi*. To help readers understand the meaning and function of the expressions compiled, each one is presented as follows: (1) the original expression in Arabic, (2) a transliteration of the Arabic to aid pronunciation or for those who cannot read Arabic script, (3) a literal translation to give the precise meaning of the original, (4) an English equivalent or explanation to indicate how they might be used in real life. They are grouped according to their linguistic function, such as criticism, warning, or advice, to guide readers as to when and how they are used.

The colloquial Egyptian relative pronoun *2illi* is, in and of itself, worthy of note. *2illi* is unique as the only relative pronoun that exists in colloquial Egyptian Arabic despite its many equivalents in Modern Standard Arabic (*2allazi*, *2allati*, *2allazaan*, *2allataan*, *2allazayn*, *2allatayn*, *2allaziina*, and *2allaati*) or in English (who, which, that, whom, whose, where, and when). The sheer number of idiomatic phrases and proverbs that start with *2illi* is quite remarkable, making it one of the most frequently used pronouns by native speakers. This plethora of expressions is mirrored by their broad spectrum of meaning and linguistic function, covering everything from criticism and warning to appreciation and encouragement.

Understanding the various uses of the pronoun *2illi* is essential for foreign language learners of Egyptian Arabic who aspire to reach a native-like level of proficiency in both the comprehension and production of spoken Egyptian Arabic. This book will prove to be a useful tool in pursuit of this aim, as mastery of idioms is arguably one of the trickiest aspects of learning a new language. Learners of English as a foreign language will also benefit from this book, thanks to the inclusion of equivalent expressions and translations into English, and it will help students master the idiomatic vocabulary of English.

Pronunciation Guide

Consonants

2   a glottal stop, as in the middle of "uh-oh!"

3   the guttural letter "ayn," pronounced with a constriction far back in the throat, rather like a backward gulp; if you can't manage it, substitute it with an "α" (see below)

7   a 'heavy' h, pronounced in the back of the throat, like the sound you might make when you step into an unexpectedly cold shower

D   an emphatic "d," pronounced with the tongue bunched up in the back of the mouth

S   an emphatic "s," pronounced with the tongue bunched up in the back of the mouth

T   an emphatic "t," pronounced with the tongue bunched up in the back of the mouth

g   always a hard "g," as in "get"

sh   as in the word "ship"

kh   like the "ch" in the German "Bach" or the Scottish pronunciation of "loch"

gh   pronounced like "kh," but with the vocal cords vibrating

Doubled consonants indicate a sound pronounced for a slightly longer time: think of the stress on the "k" sound in "bookcase" or on the "m" sound in "home-maker."

Vowels

Doubled vowels indicate long vowel sounds.

a   like the "a" in "hat"
a   like the "a" in the American pronunciation of "also" or the *o* in British pronunciation of "hot"
e   like the "ai" in "wait"
i   like the "i" in "fish"
ou   like the "ou" in "mourning"
oo   like the "ow" in "own"
u   like the "u" in "put"

Sarcasm

اللي أعطاك يعطينا

2illi 2a3Taak yi3Tiina

Whatever God gave to you,
he will give to us too

**Don't be arrogant about
your own good fortune**

اللي معاه قرش محيّره
يجيب حمام ويطيّره

2illi ma3aah 2irshi-m7ayyaru
yigiib 7amaam wiy-Tayyaru

If you don't know what to
do with your money, buy
pigeons and let them fly

**You have more
money than sense**

اللي ياكل لوحده يزور

2illi yaakul liwa7du yizwar

When you eat alone, you choke

Sharing is caring

اللي يلاقي اللي يطبخ له، ليه يحرق صوابعه؟

2illi-ylaa2i-lli yuTbukhlu leh yi7ra2 Sawab3u

Why burn your fingers if you have someone to cook for you?

You don't have to do your own dirty work if you can find someone else to do it

اللي حضّر العفريت يعرف يصرفه

2illi 7aDDar il3afriit yi3raf yiSrifu

If you can summon a ghost,
you can dismiss it

**You made your bed, now
you have to lie in it**

اللي ما تعرفش ترقص
تقول الأرض عوجة

2illi mati3rafsh tur2uS
ti2uuli-l2arDi-3ooga

She who doesn't know how to
dance says the floor is crooked

**Excuses are merely
nails used to build a
house of failure**

اللي معاه قرش
يساوي قرش

2illi ma3aah 2irsh yisaawi 2irsh

You have a penny, you're
worth a penny

Money talks

Criticism

اللي بيته من إزاز
مايحدفش الناس بالطوب

2illi betu min 2izaaz
mayi7difshi-nnaas biTTuub

If your house is made of glass, you
shouldn't throw stones at people

**People in glasshouses
shouldn't throw stones**

اللي اختشوا ماتوا

2illi-khtashu maatu

Those who fear shame
have all died

Have you no shame?

اللي بيقول مابيعملش
واللي بيعمل مابيقولش

2illi biy2uul mabyi3milsh
willi-byi3mil mabiy2ulsh

Those who speak don't act, and
those who act don't speak

**Actions speak louder
than words**

اللي على راسه بطحة
بيحسّس عليها

*2illi 3ala raasu baT7a
biy7assis 3aleha*

If you have a bump on the
head, you'll keep touching it

If the shoe fits, wear it

اللي مايعرفش يقول عدس

2illi mayi3rafshi-y2uul 3ats

If you don't know, just say "lentils"

You're talking through your hat

اللي يعيش ياما يشوف

2illi-y3iish yaama-yshuuf

The longer you live,
the more you see

You live and learn

Warnings

اللي يزرع خير يلاقي خير
واللي يزرع شر يلاقي شر

*2illi yizra3 kher yilaa2i kher
willi yizra3 sharri-ylaa2i sharr*

Plant good deeds and you'll get
good deeds, plant evil deeds
and you'll get evil deeds

You reap what you sow

اللي ياكل على ضرسه ينفع نفسه

*2illi yaakul 3ala dirsu
yinfa3 nafsu*

You do yourself a favor when you
chew with your own molars

**Only you can
help yourself**

اللي يخاف من العفريت يطلع له

2illi yikhaaf mil-3afriit yiTla3lu

If you fear the demon, it
will appear to you

**The more you fear
something, the more
likely it will happen**

اللى اطلسع من الشوربة

ينفخ فى الزبادى

اللي اتلسع من الشوربة
ينفخ في الزبادي

*2illi-tlasa3 mishshurba
yunfukh fizzabaadi*

If you get burned by soup, you'll
start blowing on yogurt

Once bitten, twice shy

اللى بيشيل قربة مخرومة بتفضّل على دماغة

اللي بيشيل قربة مخرومة
بتخرّ على دماغه

*2illi biyshiil 2irba makhruuma
bitkhurri-3ala-dmaaghu*

Carry a punctured water bottle,
and it will drip on your head

**The chickens have
come home to roost**

يطلع فرحون | اللي تحسبه موسى

اللي تحسبه موسى
يطلع فرعون

2illi ti7sibu mousa
yiTla3 far3oon

You thought he was Moses, but
he turned out to be the Pharaoh

**Don't judge a book
by its cover**

اللي له أول له آخر

2illi luh 2awwil luh 2aakhir

That which has a
beginning has an end

**If you start
something, finish it**

اللي يلعب بالنار تحرقه

2illi yil3ab binnaar ti7ra2u

Play with fire and you
will get burned

Don't play with fire

اللي يبصّ لعيشة غيره
تحرم عليه عيشته

*2illi-ybuSSi-l3iishit gheru
ti7ram 3aleeh 3ishtu*

If you envy others, you don't
deserve your own life

**The grass is always
greener**

اللي يجي بالساهل يروح بالساهل

*2illi yiigi-bissaahil
yiruu7 bissaahil*

What is easily obtained
will be easily lost

Easy come, easy go

اللي ما تربّيه الأهالي
تربّيه الأيام والليالي

2illi matrabbii-l2ahaali tirabbii-l2ayyaam wil-layaali

If your parents didn't raise you right, you'll be raised by the days and nights

You'll learn about life the hard way

Advice

اللي مالكش فيه ماتتحشرش فيه

2illi malaksh fii matit7ishirsh fii

If it doesn't concern you,
don't meddle with it

Don't poke your nose into other people's business

اللى تعرفه احسن   من اللى ماتعرفوش

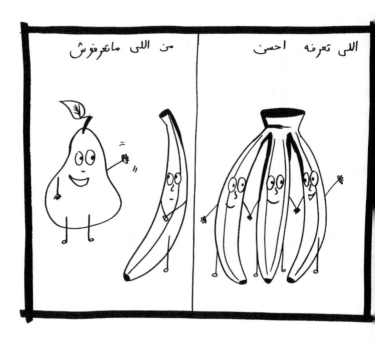

اللي تعرفه أحسن من اللي ماتعرفوش

2illi ti3rafu 2a7san milli-mati3rafuush

The person you know is better than the person you don't know

Keep your friends close and your enemies closer

اللي يقدّم السبت يلاقي الحد قدّامه

2illi-y2addimi-ssabt yilaa2i-l7addi-2uddaamu

He who helps on a Saturday
will receive help on Sunday

**You scratch my back,
and I'll scratch yours**

اللي يحب العسل
يستحمل قرص النحل

2illi-y7ibbi-l3asal
yista7mil 2arSi-nna7l

If you like honey, you must be
ready to be stung by bees

**There is no pleasure
without pain**

اللي يحتاجه البيت يحرم على الجامع

2illi yi7taagu-lbet
yi7ram 3a-ggaami3

If it's needed at home,
it's forbidden to donate
it to a mosque

Charity begins at home

اللى يصبر ...... ينول

اللي يصبر ينول

2illi yuSbur yinuul

Be patient and you'll
get what you want

Good things come
to those who wait

اللي يعمل جميل يتمّه

2illi yi3mil gimiil yittimu

If you do a favor, do it fully

**If you do a favor,
see it through**

اللي يِدُقّ يتعب

2illi-yidu22-yit3ab

If you pay too much attention,
you will exhaust yourself

Don't be too picky

اللي أوله شرط آخره نور

2illi 2awwilu sharT 2akhru nuur

Lay out your terms from the
beginning and they will be fruitful

**Take care to dot your
i's and cross your t's**

اللي تغلب بُه العب بُه

2illi tighlibbu-l3abbu

If you have a winning card, play it

Play your cards right

اللي تكره وشّه
يحوجك الزمان لقفاه

*2illi tikrah wishshu yi7wigaki-
zzamaan li2afaah*

If you hate their faces now,
you will need the back
of their heads later

Don't burn your bridges

اللي ماعهوش مايلزموش

2illi ma3ahuush mayilzamuush

If you can't afford it,
you don't need it

**Cut your coat according
to your cloth**

Empathizing and Consoling

اللي مكتوب على الجبين
لازم تشوفه العين

2illi maktuub 3al-gibiin
laazim tishuufu-l3en

What is written on the forehead
will inevitably be seen by the eye

Fate will find a way

اللي انكسر يتصلّح

2illi-nkasar yitSalla7

What is broken can be fixed

Nothing is beyond repair

اللي فات مات

2illi faat maat

The past is dead

Let bygones be bygones

اللي تخاف منه ما
يجيش أحسن منه

*2illi-tkhaaf minnu
maygiisha-7san minnu*

That which you fear will
turn out to be the best

Face your fears

اللي جاي أحسن من اللي راح

2illi gayya-7san milli-raa7

What is coming is better
than what has passed

**Tomorrow will be
better than today**

Rebuke, Regret, Threats

اللي مش عاجبه يشرب من البحر

*2illi mish 3agbu
yishrab mil-ba7r*

If you don't like it, drink
from the sea

If you don't like it, lump it

اللي إيده في الميّة مش
زي اللي إيده في النار

*2illi 2idu fil-mayya mish
zayyi-lli 2idu finnaar*

Hands in water aren't the
same as hands in fire

**Don't judge someone
until you have walked
a mile in their shoes**

اللي حسبته لقيته

2illi 7asabtu la2etu

I found what I had expected

My fears have come true

اللي يرشني بالميّة أرشه بالدم

2illi-yrushshini bilmayya
2arushshu biddamm

If someone sprays me with water,
I will spray them with blood

**I will hit back
twice as hard**

اللي يقول لمراته يا عورة الناس تلعب بيها الكورة

2illi-y2uul limraatu ya 3oora-nnaas til3ab-biiha-kkoora

If a man calls his wife one-eyed, people will play her like a soccer ball

Don't disrespect your wife in public or others will disrespect her too

Appreciation and Encouragement

اللي على البر عوّام

2illi 3al-barri-3awwaam

Whoever reaches the shore
is a master swimmer

Don't be a backseat driver

اللي يبص لي بعين
أبص له بالاتنين

2illi-ybuSSi-lib-3en
2abuSSi-lub-litnen

If you look at me with one eye, I
will look at you with both eyes

A favor for a favor

اللي سبق أكل النبق

2illi saba2 2akali-nnaba2

Whoever came first
ate the buckthorn

**The early bird
catches the worm**

Printed in the USA
CPSIA information can be obtained
at www.ICGtesting.com
JSHW060716290224
57956JS00001B/1

9 781649 033468